AF583746

Teacher's note: Have children trace over the letter and colour the picture when the study of the focus letter is complete.

Channel

Trace over

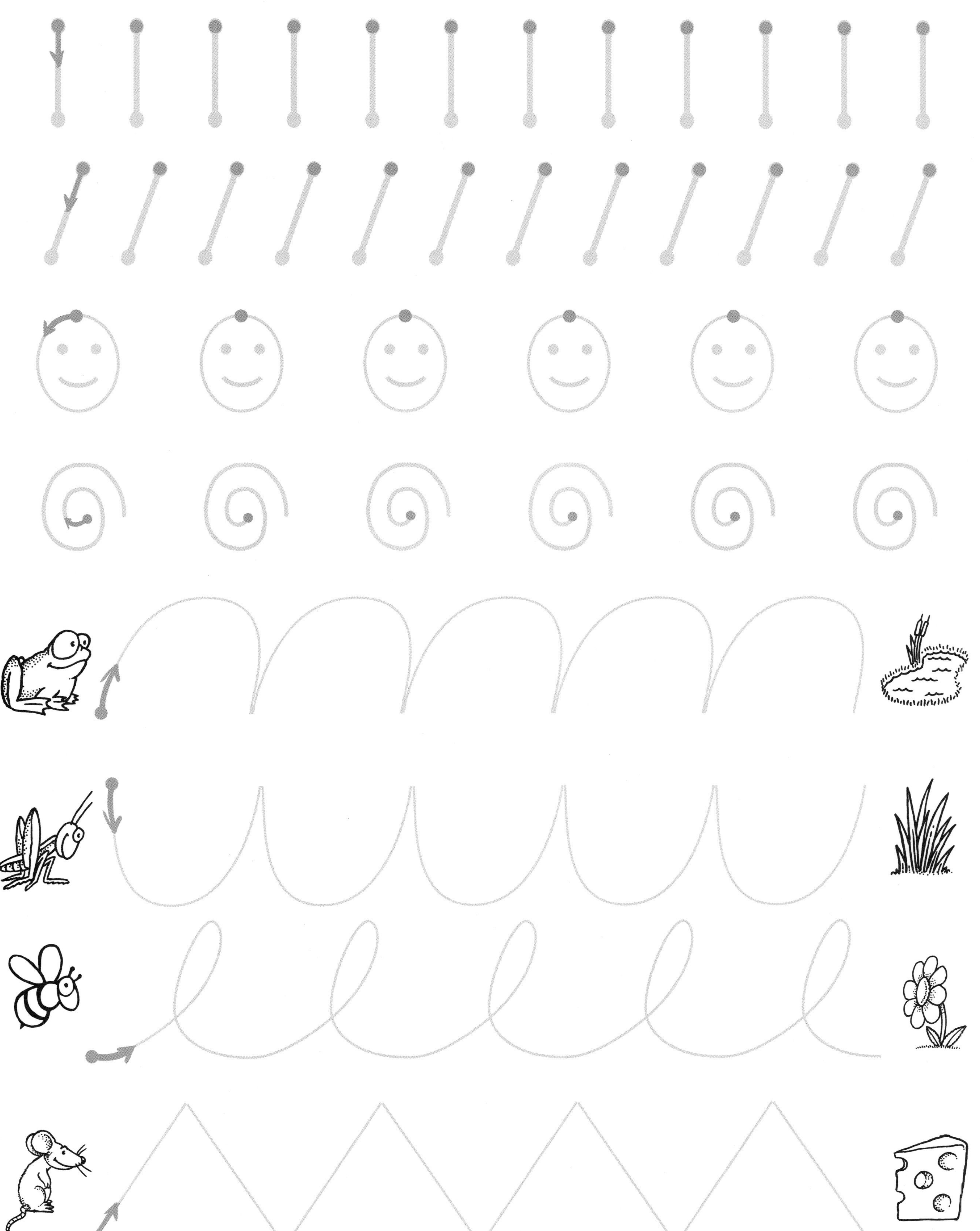

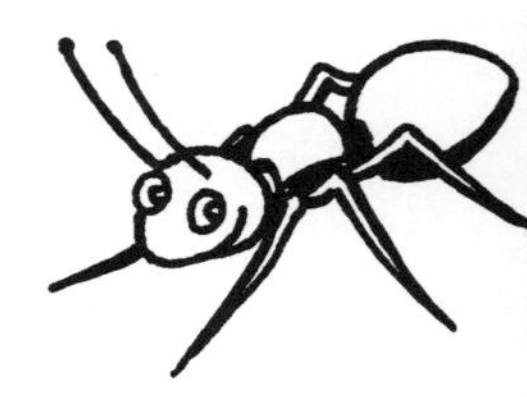

Channel

a a a a a

Trace over

a a a a a

Copy

a

Trace over

ant ant ant

Aa

Bb

Channel

Trace over

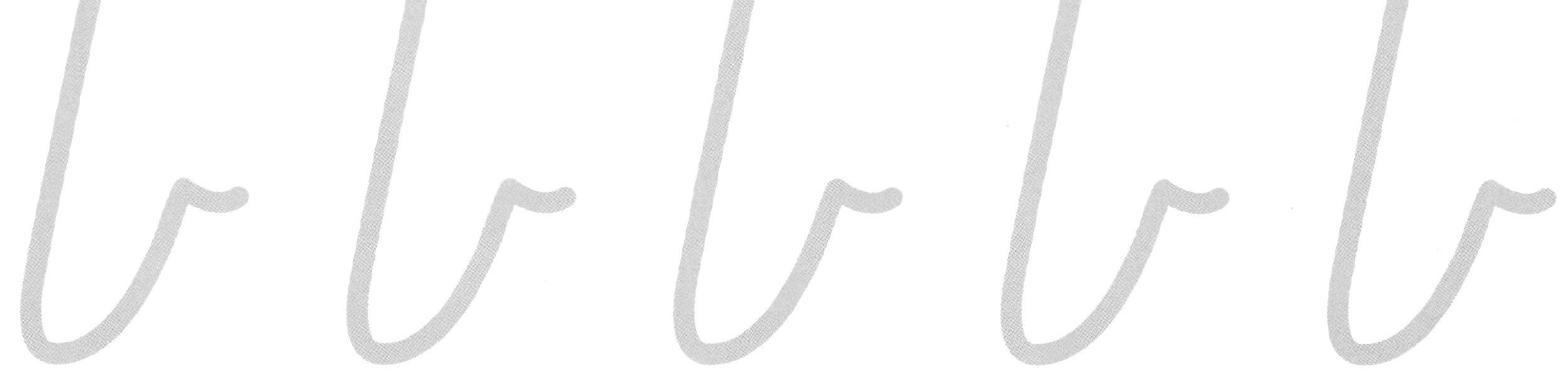

Copy

b

Trace over

bee bee bee

Channel

Trace over

c c c c c

Copy

c

Trace over

cake cake

Cc

Dd

Channel

d d d d d

Trace over

d d d d d

Copy

d

Trace over

dog dog dog

Channel

  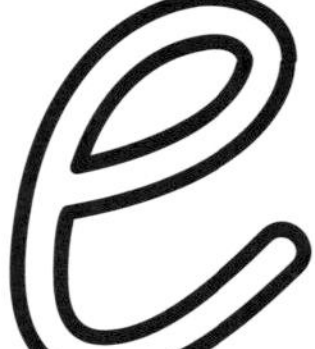 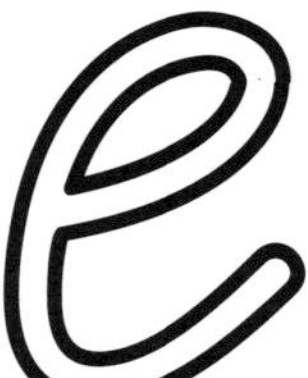 

Trace over

e e e e e

Copy

e

Trace over

ears ears ears

Ee

Ff

f

Channel

Trace over

Copy

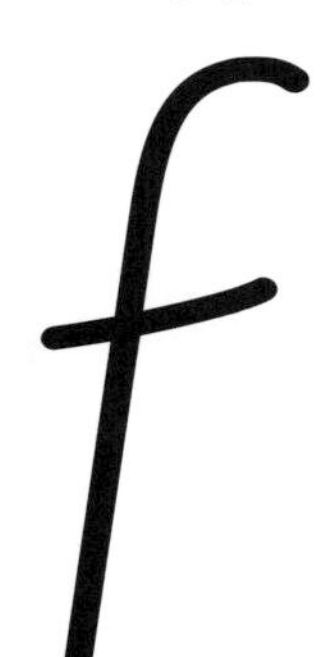

Trace over

foot foot

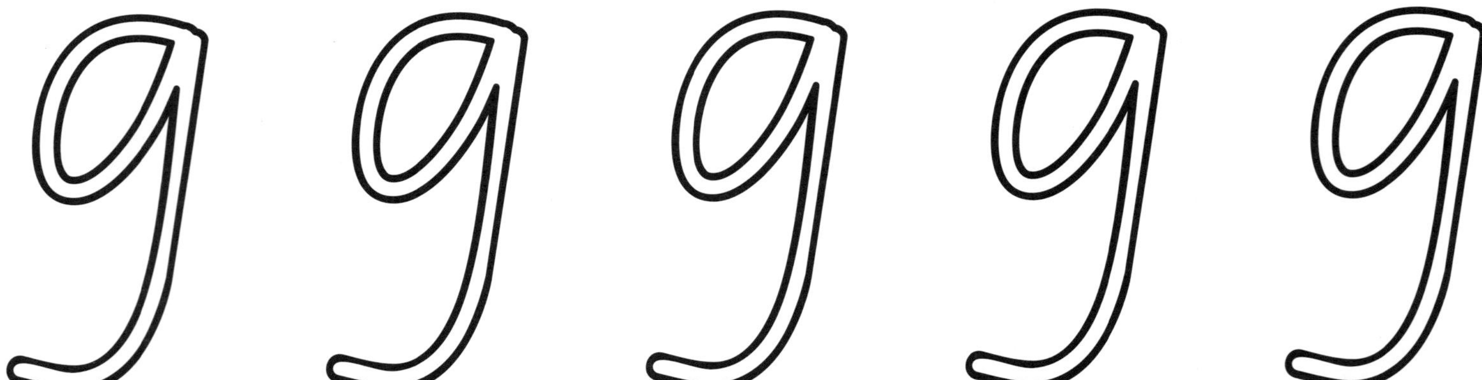

Trace over

g g g g g

Copy

g

Trace over

goat goat

Gg

Hh

Channel

Trace over

h h h h h

Copy

h

Trace over

hand hand

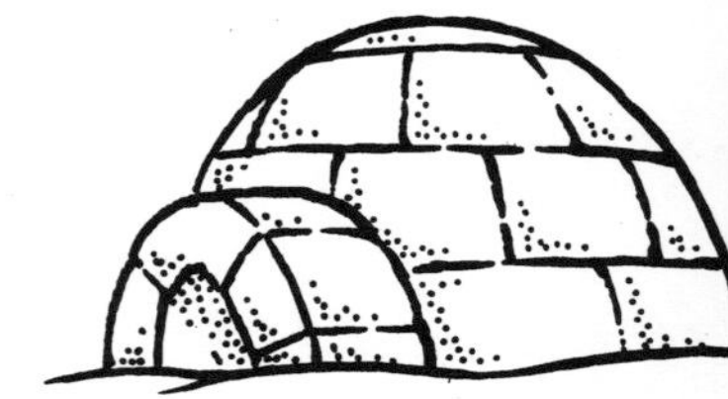

Channel

i i i i i

Trace over

i i i i i

Copy

i

Trace over

igloo igloo

Ii

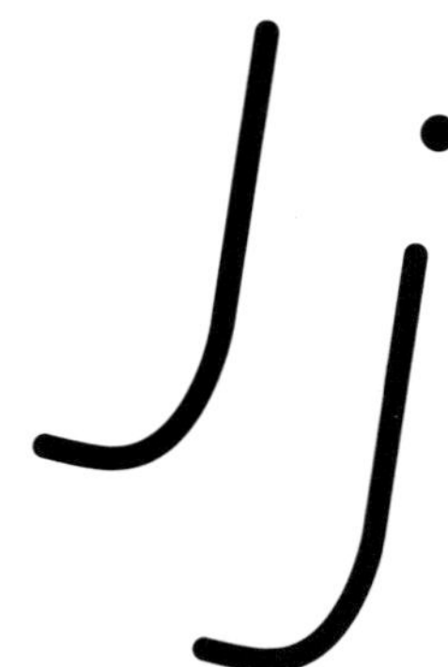

Channel

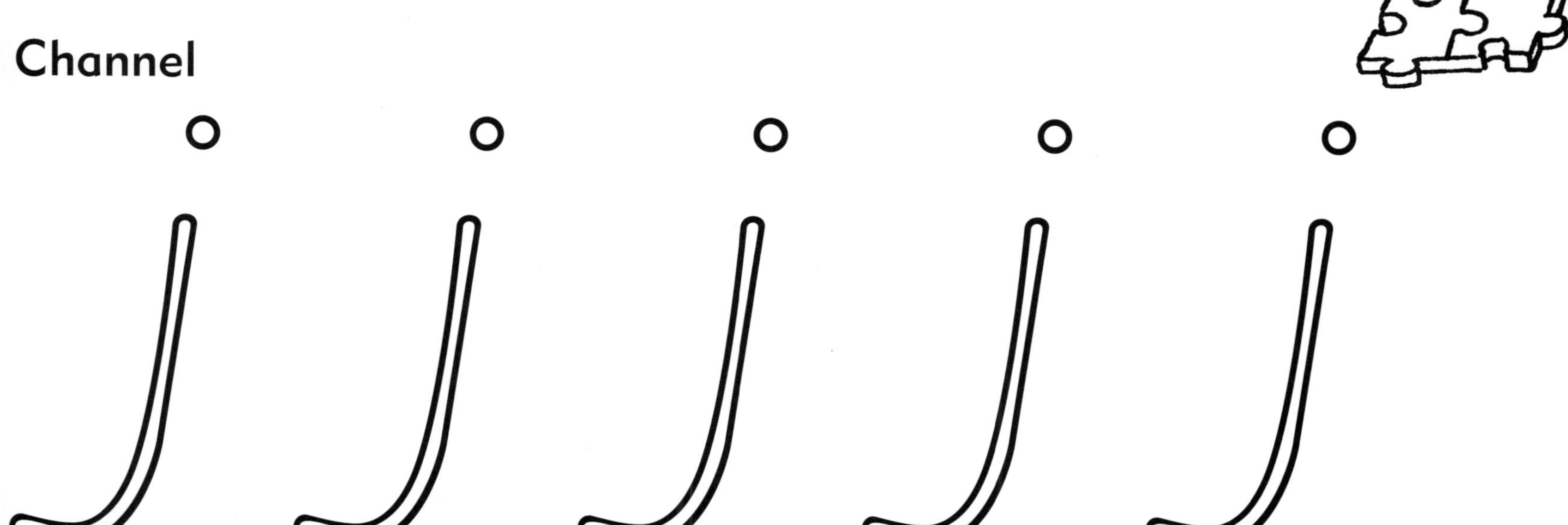

Trace over

Copy

Trace over

jigsaw jigsaw

Channel

Trace over

Copy

Trace over

king king

Kk

Ll

Channel

l l l l l

Trace over

l l l l l

Copy

l

Trace over

lips lips lips

Channel

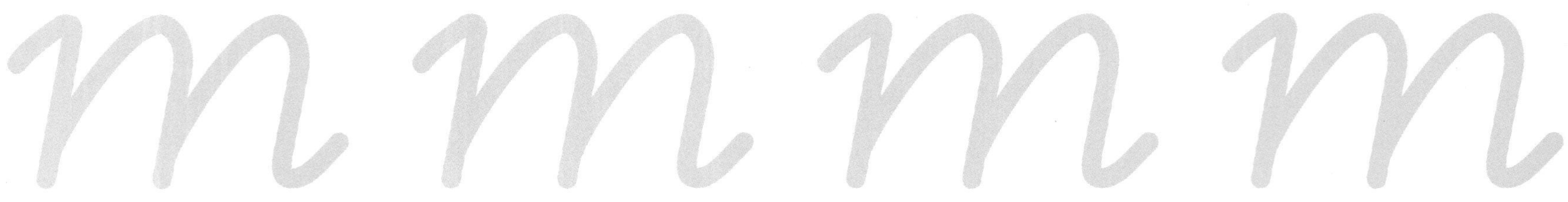

Trace over

m m m m

Copy

m

Trace over

mouse mouse

Mm

m

Nn

Channel

n n n n n

Trace over

Copy

n

Trace over

nest nest

Channel

 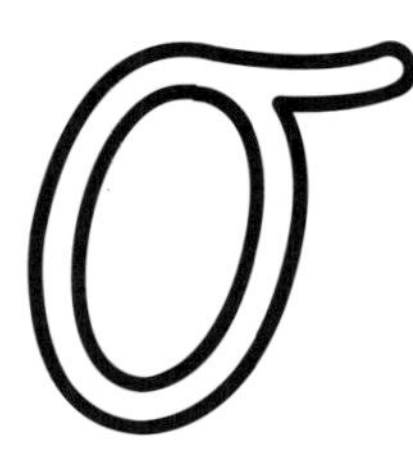  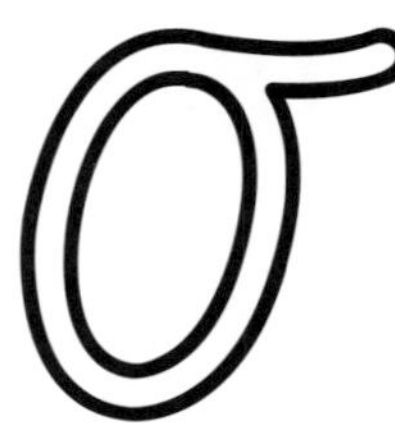 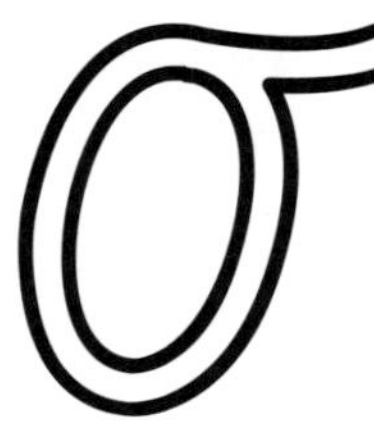

Trace over

o o o o o

Copy

Trace over

octopus octopus

Ορ σ

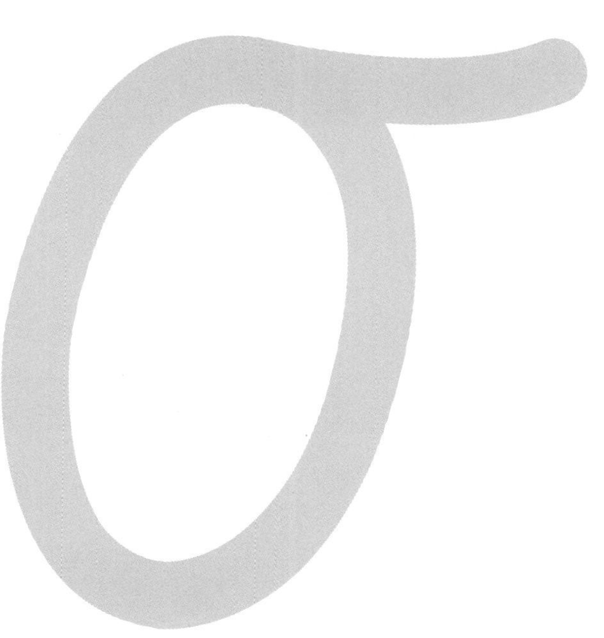

Pp

Channel

p p p p p

Trace over

p p p p p

Copy

Trace over

pig pig pig

Channel

q q q q q

Trace over

q q q q q

Copy

q

Trace over

queen queen

Qq

Rr

Channel

r r r r r

Trace over

r r r r r

Copy

r

Trace over

rabbit rabbit

Channel

s s s s s s

Trace over

s s s s s s

Copy

s

Trace over

snake snake

Ss

Tt

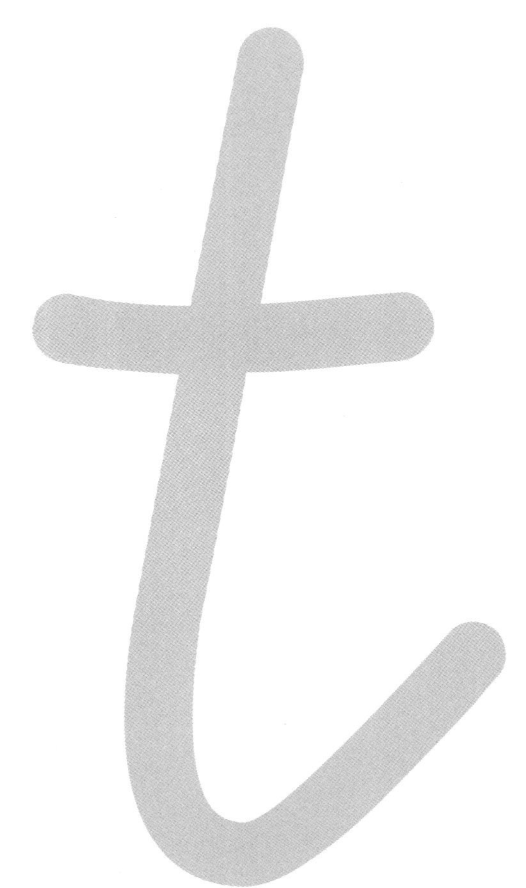

Channel

t t t t t

Trace over

t t t t t

Copy

t

Trace over

tent tent

Channel

u u u u u

Trace over

u u u u u

Copy

u

Trace over

umbrella umbrella

Uu

Vv

Channel

v v v v v

Trace over

v v v v v

Copy

v

Trace over

vet vet vet

Channel

w w w w

Trace over

w w w w

Copy

w

Trace over

wand wand

Ww

Xx

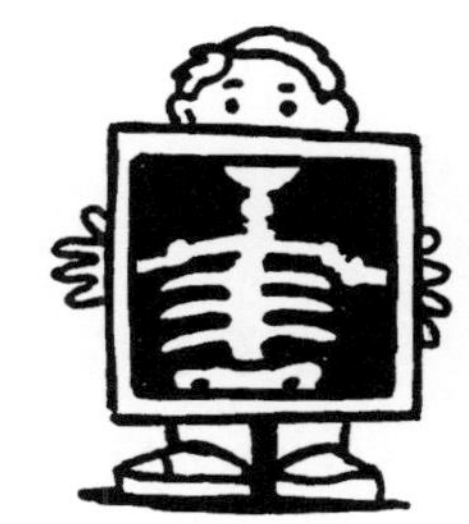

Channel

x x x x

Trace over

x x x x

Copy

x

Trace over

x-ray x-ray

Channel

y y y y y

Trace over

y y y y y

Copy

y

Trace over

yacht yacht

Yy

Z ʒ

Channel

z z z z z

Trace over

z z z z z

Copy

z

Trace over

zebra zebra

Find and trace over the letters of the alphabet. Colour the picture.